Other cat books by Exley:
Cats and other Crazy Cuddlies   The Fanatic's Guide to Cats
Cat Quotations   The Crazy World of Cats
The Illustrated Cat Address Book The Cat Notebook

Published simultaneously in 1992 by Exley Publications
Ltd. in Great Britain, and Exley Giftbooks in the USA.
Selection and arrangement © Helen Exley 1992
ISBN 1-85015-328-0
Reprinted 1992 (twice), 1993 (twice)

A copy of the CIP data is available from the British
Library on request.

Edited by Helen Exley
Designed by Pinpoint Design Company
Typeset by Delta, Watford.
Printed in Hungary.
Exley Publications Ltd, 16 Chalk Hill, Watford, Herts WD1 4BN,
United Kingdom.
Exley Giftbooks, 359 East Main Street, Suite 3D, Mount Kisco, 10549, USA.

Picture Credits: AKG: 39; Bridgeman Art Library: cover; Mary Evans;
Explorer; Peter Kettle; Scala.
The publishers would like to thank the following for permission to reproduce
copyright material. They would be pleased to hear from any copyright
holders not here acknowledged.
"Cats" by Eleanor Farjeon, reprinted by permission of David Higham
Associates Ltd; extract from "Esther's Tom Cat" by Ted Hughes from
Lupercal, reprinted by permission of the publihsers, Faber and Faber Ltd;
extract from The Purr-fect Cat Book by Isha Mellor, reprinted by permission
of the publishers, Piatkus Books Ltd; extract from "Catalogue" by Rosalie
Moore, reprinted by permission; © 1940, 1968 The New Yorker Magazine,
Inc.; extract from "Miss Tibbles" by Ian Serraillier, reprinted by permission
of the author.

CATS

A CELEBRATION
IN WORDS
AND PAINTINGS

SELECTED BY
HELEN EXLEY

EXLEY
MT. KISCO, NEW YORK • WATFORD, UK

WHAT LIFE IS ALL ABOUT

Often, when I have been feeling lonely, when a book has been thrust aside in boredom, when the keys of the piano, softly lit, hold no invitation to the dance, I have lain back and stared at the shadows on the ceiling, wondering what life is all about . . . and then, suddenly, there is the echo of the swinging door, and across the carpet, walking with the utmost delicacy and precision, stalks "Four" or "Five" or Oscar. He sits down on the floor beside me, regarding my long legs, my old jumper, and my floppy arms, with a purely practical interest. Which part of this large male body will form the most appropriate lap? Usually he settles for the chest. Whereupon he springs up and there is a feeling of cold fur - for the night is frosty - and the tip of an icy nose, thrust against my wrist and a positive tattoo of purrs. And I no longer wonder what life is all about.

BEVERLEY NICHOLS

>‹

HONOURABLE CAT

I am Cat.
I am honourable.
I have pride.
I have dignity.
And I have memory.
For I am older than you.
I am older than your Gods; the Tree Gods,
the Stone Gods,
The thunder and Lightning and the Sun Gods
And your God of Love
I too can love
But with only half a heart
And that I offer you.
Accept what I am able to give
For were I to give you all
I could not bear your inevitable treachery.
Let us remain honourable friends.

PAUL GALLICO (1896-1976)
FROM *"HONOURABLE CAT"*

ON KITTENS

A kitten is the delight of a household.
All day long a comedy is played out by an
incomparable actor.

CHAMPFLEURY (1821-1899)

The kitten was six weeks old. It was
enchanting, a delicate fairy-tale cat, whose
Siamese genes showed in the shape of the
face, ears, tail, and the subtle lines of its
body. . . . From the front, sitting with her
slender paws straight, she was an exotically
beautiful beast. She sat, a tiny thing, in the
middle of a yellow carpet, surrounded by five
worshippers, not at all afraid of us. Then
she stalked around that floor of the house,
inspecting every inch of it, climbed up on to
my bed, crept under the fold of a sheet, and
was at home.

DORIS LESSING, b. 1919

SHEER BEAUTY

A cat is beautiful at a distance - near-to he is an inexhaustible matter for wonder: the patterning of his eyes, the elaborations of his ears, the beautiful precision of his nostrils, the elaborate whorls of his face fur, the elegance of his bones, the delicacy of his sinews, the efficiency of his paws, the separate aliveness of his tail. His mouth is incredibly clean, incredibly pink. His teeth are precision made. The roof is rippled, his tongue rasped. Everything he does is a perfection.

PAM BROWN, b.1928

The smallest feline is a masterpiece.

LEONARDO DA VINCI

Oh cat: I'd say, or pray: be-*oooo*tiful cat!
Delicious cat! Exquisite cat! Satiny cat!
Cat like a soft owl, cat with paws like moths,
jewelled cat, miraculous cat!
Cat, cat, cat, cat.

DORIS LESSING, b. 1919

The flowers think they are
more beautiful than we,
But they are wrong.

PAUL GALLICO

MEMORIES OF CALVIN

We understood each other perfectly, but we never made any fuss about it; when I spoke his name and snapped my fingers, he came to me; when I returned home at night, he was pretty sure to be waiting for me near the gate, and would rise and saunter along the walk, as if his being there was purely accidental - so shy was he commonly of showing feeling. There was one thing he never did - he never rushed through an open doorway.

He never forgot his dignity. If he had asked to have the door opened; and was eager to go out, he always went out deliberately; I can see him now, standing on the sill, looking about at the sky as if he was thinking whether it was worthwhile to take an umbrella, until he was near having his tail shut in.

CHARLES DUDLEY WARNER (1898-1976)

THE GARDENER'S CAT

The gardener's cat's called Mignonette,
She hates the cold, she hates the wet,
She sits among the hothouse flowers
And sleeps for hours and hours and hours.

····•• •••··

She dreams she is a tiger fierce
With great majestic claws that pierce,
She sits by the hot-water pipes
And dreams about a coat of stripes;

····•• •••··

And in her slumbers she will go
And stalks the sullen buffalo,
And then he roars across the brake
She does not wink, she does not wake.

·····• •·····

It must be perfectly immense
To dream with such magnificence,
And pass the most inclement day
In this indeed stupendous way.

·····• •·····

She dreams of India's sunny clime,
And only wakes at dinnertime,
And even then she does not stir
But waits till milk is brought to her.

·····• •·····

How nice to be the gardener's cat,
She troubles not for mouse or rat,
But, when it's coming down in streams,
She sits among the flowers and dreams.

·····• •·····

The gardener's cat would be the thing,
Her dreams are so encouraging;
She dreams that she's a tiger, yet
She's just a cat called Mignonette!

PATRICK R. CHALMERS

➤ ❖ ❮

CONFESSION

I've been named Poosie, and
I am spoiled
Thoroughly, thoroughly spoiled, and I like it.
And don't let anyone tell you different.
I lie upon the softest cushions,
Under the downiest covers
And love every moment.
I get the cream off the top of the milk every day
And special double thick, heavy on Sundays,
And I lap it up.
My owner is besotted.
She hugs and kisses me
And carries me around with her all day,
And talks to me and I enjoy it.
I'm spoiled rotten, and, friends,
That's the life.
Whatever I want, I cry for,
Crab, lobster, caviare, fish roes, sardines, fillet,
white meat of chicken,
You name it, she's got it,
I get it.
I don't want to work, or hunt.

If ten snow-white mice were to saunter past
my nose,
I wouldn't lift a paw.
I'm greedy, graceless, shameless, lazy,
And luxury loving.
Everything that comes my way I take,
And yell for more.
I'm spoiled useless.
I admit it.
And I adore it.

PAUL GALLICO
(1896-1976)

KITTEN VERSES

A kitten with a length of string
Is such a pretty, playful thing.
A kitten with a leaf to chase
Exhibits beauty, form and grace.
But I love kittens curled up, wise,
With ancient mystery in their eyes.

SALVATORE MARSIGLIA

I wish she wouldn't ask me if
I love the kitten more than her.
Of course I love her -
But I love the kitten too, And it has fur. . .

ANON

I like little Pussy, her coat is so warm,
And if I don't hurt her, she'll do me no harm.
So I'll not pull her tail, nor drive her away,
But Pussy and I very gently will play.

SOURCE UNKNOWN, c.1843

CAT ON THE HEARTH

The firelight flickers on the Chinese tray
And on the books set snugly in their rack;
Copper and silver flow beneath its play,
The chairs are placed - what is it that we lack?

····•• •••··

She comes. With each foot delicately placed,
Advancing like a vestal to the rite,
She scorns to move with unbecoming haste
Or note the lesser objects in her sight.

····•• •••··

She settles couchant; curves one placid paw
Beneath her chest; now curves its mate
the same;
Yields to the promptings of some ancient law
And fastens thoughtful eyes upon the flame.

····•• •••··

Now let the night wind rise, the grey storm
come.
The cat is on the hearth - we are at home.

SILENCE BUCK BELLOWS

✢

WHO OWNS WHO?

I'd like to think I owned the cat
That condescends to share my flat;
I give him of my rationed food
And cater to his every mood.
I'd like to think he'd go to seed
If I weren't there to meet his need,
And yet the fact is plain to see -
The pesky, doggone cat owns me!

RUTH M. OUTWATER

Dogs will play football, walk a tightrope,
and do backflips; bears will roller-skate
or ride seesaws, and seals render "My
Country 'Tis of Thee" on a bank of tooters,
but your pet cat won't even come when
you call it if it doesn't feel like it or doesn't
think there might be something in it
for itself.

PAUL GALLICO (1896-1976)

WHAT IS A CAT?

The house-cat is a four-legged quadruped, the legs as usual being at the corners. It is what is sometimes called a tame animal, though it feeds on mice and birds of prey. Its colours are striped, it does not bark, but breathes through its nose instead of its mouth. Cats also mow, which you all have heard. Cats have nine liveses, but which is seldom wanted in this country, coz' of Christianity. Cats eat meat and most anythink speshuelly where you can't afford. That is all about cats.

A SCHOOLBOY'S ESSAY, 1903

A cat is a Regency gentleman – elegant of pose, exquisite of manner, with spotless linen and an enthusiasm for bare knuckle fights, rampaging love affairs, duels by moonlight and the singing of glees. He expects immaculate service from his domestic staff, and possesses a range of invective that would make a navvy blanch.

PAM BROWN

Another World

A cat's eyes are windows enabling us to see into another world.

IRISH LEGEND

Lift up your large black satin eyes which are like cushions where one sinks! Fawn at my feet, fantastic Sphinx! and sing me all your memories!

OSCAR WILDE (1856-1900)

He shut his eyes while Saha (the cat) kept vigil, watching all the invisible signs that hover over sleeping human beings when the light is out.

FROM *"THE CAT"*, 1933

✦

Daylong this tomcat lies stretched flat
As an old rough mat, no mouth and no eyes.
Continual wars and wives are what
Have tattered his ears and battered his head.

••• •••

Like a bundle of old rope and iron
Sleeps till blue dusk. Then reappear
His eyes, green as ringstones: he yawns wide red,
Fangs fine as a lady's needle and bright.

••• •••

. . . He leaps and lightly
Walks upon sleep, his mind on the moon.
Nightly over the round world of men,
Over the roofs go his eyes and outcry.

TED HUGHES, b. 1930
"ESTHER'S TOMCAT"

✦

BEWARE OF THE CAT

We tie bright ribbons around their necks,
and occasionally little tinkling bells, and we
affect to think that they are as sweet and
vapid as the coy name "kitty" by which we call
them would imply. It is a curious illusion. For,
purring beside our fireplaces and pattering
along our back fences, we have got a wild
beast as uncowed and uncorrupted
as any under heaven.

ALAN DEVOE

When I grow up I mean to be
A Lion large and fierce to see.
I'll mew so loud that Cook in fright
Will give me all the cream in sight.
And anyone who dares to say
"Poor Puss" to me will rue the day.
Then having swallowed him I'll creep
Into the Guest Room Bed to sleep.

OLIVER HERFORD (AFTER R.L.S.)

The last thing I would accuse a cat
of is innocence.

EDWARD PALEY (1786-1847)

When a cat is offended every square centimetre
of him is offended. Men and women of power
and intellect have been brought to their knees
by cats who have turned their backs on them.

A. P. REILLY

INSTINCT

"Japanese goldfish,
With your gossamer tail,
You are the loveliest creature
I have ever seen."

"Japanese kitten,
Put your tongue back in where it belongs
And go away.
I know exactly what you are thinking."

PAUL GALLICO (1896-1976)

Sunday, January 27 1884 - There was another
story in the paper a week or so since. A
gentleman had a favourite cat whom he taught
to sit at the dinner table where it behaved very
well. He was in the habit of putting any scraps
he left on to the cat's plate. One day puss did
not take his place punctually, but presently
appeared with two mice, one of which it placed
on its master's plate, the other on its own.

BEATRIX POTTER (1866-1943)

THE CAT AND THE MOON

The cat went here and there
And the moon spun round like a top
And the nearest kin of the moon,
The creeping cat, looked up.
Black Minnaloushe stared at the moon,
For, wander and wail as he would,
The pure cold light in the sky
Troubled his animal blood.
Minnaloushe runs in the grass
Lifting his delicate feet.
Do you dance, Minnaloushe, do you dance?
When two close kindred meet,
What better than call a dance?
Maybe the moon may learn,
Tired of that courtly fashion
A new dance turn.

Minnaloushe creeps through the grass
From moonlit place to place,
The sacred moon overhead
has taken a new phase.
Does Minnaloushe know that his pupils
Will pass from change to change,
And that from round to crescent,
From crescent to round they range?
Minnaloushe creeps through the grass
Alone, important and wise,
And lifts to the changing moon
his changing eyes.

W. B. YEATS (1865-1939)

→←

OFF TO SLEEP . . .

When I am cosied into sleep
my cat demands the door,
but when at last I'm warm again
he hammers on the window pane
- and I am up once more,
open the casement, see him leap,
Nijinsky, from the ledge;
a ghost of leaves and night and rain
he settles on the counterpane;
and I am left the edge.

PAM BROWN, b.1928

I don't mind a cat, in its place. But its place is
not in the middle of my back at 4 a.m.

MAYNARD GOOD STODDARD

In the morning, when she wishes me to wake,
she crouches on my chest, and pats my face with
her paw. Or, if I am on my side, she crouches
looking into my face. Soft, soft touches of her paw.

I open my eyes, say I don't want to wake. I close my eyes. Cat gently pats my eyelids. Cat licks my nose. Cat starts purring, two inches from my face. Cat, then, as I lie pretending to be asleep, delicately bites my nose. I laugh and sit up. At which she bounds off my bed and streaks downstairs - to have the back door opened if it is winter, to be fed, if it is summer.

DORIS LESSING, b. 1919

CATS SLEEP ANYWHERE

Cats sleep
Anywhere,
Any table
Any chair,
Top of piano,
Window-ledge,
In the middle,
On the edge,
Open drawer,
Empty shoe,
Anybody's
Lap will do,
Fitted in a
Cardboard box,
In the cupboard
With your frocks -
Anywhere!
They don't care!
Cats sleep
Anywhere.

ELEANOR FARJEON (1881-1965)

Cat's cradle,
Cat's slumber,
Soft slumber;
Sleep softly
All cats. . . .

PAUL GALLICO (1896-1976)
EXTRACT FROM *"SLEEP"*

SURRENDER

Let others praise the cat
And rhapsodize
About her velvet tread
And amber eyes.
I never liked the feline.
Yet, this first cool Fall day,
Before the furnace started,
I looked out upon my door-stoop
And espied a long gray cat.
Her sinuous back was curled
Around a straying sunbeam
Which seemed to catch and hold her
In a deep and friendly dream.
The sight brought warm comfort
To my lonely flat ...
Which is a bit more cheerful ...
Now, that I have a cat.

EVELYN HICKMAN

CAT AND DOG COMPARED

The dog is a hearty beast; you can ruffle his coat, and slap him on the back, and he'll beam at you. The fastidious cat hates to have his fur mussed, and loathes any show of heartiness. You must approach him quite differently. Ceremonial is required. A man who loved and owned dogs, but had never kept a cat, once went up to my mother's Pinkle Purr, and saying "Hello, old chap! You magnificent fellow!" gave her beloved tyrant a friendly smack on the behind. A dog would have contorted with delight. Pinkle Purr gave the visitor one mighty scratch, and fled in horror, his majesty outraged. It was as though a Cockney had bawled "Wot cher, Cock!" in the Throne Room.

KATHARINE L. SIMMS

Cats cannot be made to do anything useful.

P. J. O'ROURKE

Dogs live with you, cats board with you.

PAM BROWN, b. 1928

Humans have remade dogs to suit their own ends. Cats are exactly the same as they were ten thousand years ago.

MARION C. GARRETTY, b. 1917

➔ ←

TAFFY TOPAZ

Taffy, the topaz-coloured cat,
Thinks now of this and now of that,
But chiefly of his meals.
Asparagus, and cream, and fish,
Are objects of his Freudian wish;
What you don't give, he steals.

His gallant heart is strongly stirred
By clink of plate or flight of bird,
He has a plumy tail;
At night he treads on stealthy pad
As merry as Sir Galahad
A-seeking of the Grail.

His amiable amber eyes
Are very friendly, very wise;
Like Buddha, grave and fat,
He sits, regardless of applause,
And thinking, as he kneads his paws,
What fun to be a cat!

CHRISTOPHER MORLEY

Hearths are quite the favourite place
For cats to slip into good grace:
They stretch where flames high-light their fur,
Tuning the room with soothing purr.
At charming they are extra smart,
Knowing sly wiles to win one's heart.

Undoubtedly the prudent cat
Is nature's choicest diplomat.

LEE RICHARD HAYMAN

→ ←

LORDLY FRIEND

Stately, kindly, lordly friend
Condescend
Here to sit by me and turn
Glorious eyes that smile and burn,
Golden eyes, love's lustrous meed,
On the golden page I read.

ALGERNON CHARLES SWINBURNE (1837-1909)

A cat is only technically an animal,
being divine.

ROBERT LYND (1879-1949)

Cats, as a class, have never completely
got over the snootiness caused by the fact
that in ancient Egypt they were worshipped
as gods.

P. G. WODEHOUSE (1881-1975)

In Egypt: Under no conditions, under threat of
death could anyone kill a cat. People were
executed for even killing a cat accidentally.
And when a cat died, the whole family,
and probably their closest friends, went
into mourning, the measure of their
personal loss signalled by their shaving off
their eyebrows.

ROGER A. CARAS

PURR . . .

. . . Sometimes I like her calm, unwild,
gentle as a sleeping child,

····•·•····

and wonder as she lies, a fur ring,
curled upon my lap, unstirring –
is it me or Tibbles purring?

IAN SERRAILLIER
EXTRACT FROM *"MISS TIBBLES"*

Cats make one of the most satisfying sounds in
the world: they purr. Almost all cats make us
feel good about ourselves because they let us
know they feel good about us, about themselves,
and about our relationship with them. A purring
cat is a form of high praise, like a gold star on a
test paper. It is reinforcement of something we
would all like to believe about ourselves - that
we are nice.

ROGER CARAS

A LIFE OF LUXURY

Tsar Nicholas I of Russia fed his cat, Vashka,
a celebratory concoction of the best caviare
poached in rich champagne, with finely minced
French dormouse, unsalted butter, cream,
whipped woodcock's egg and hare's blood.
Rather than trouble his servants, Doctor
Johnson himself purchased oysters for
his cat, Hodge.

DAVID TAYLOR

A cat knows how to be comfortable, how to get
the people around it to serve it. In a tranquil
domestic situation, the cat is a veritable
manipulative genius. It seeks the soft, it seeks
the warm, it prefers the quiet and it loves to be
full. It displays, when it gets its own way in
these matters, a degree of contentment we
would all like to emulate.

ROGER CARAS

THE SURE-FOOTED CAT

Cats sleep fat and walk thin.
Cats, when they sleep, slump;
When they wake, stretch and begin
Over, pulling their ribs in.
Cats walk thin.

ROSALIE MOORE, FROM *"CATALOGUE"*

If a fish is the movement of water embodied,
given shape, then cat is a diagram and pattern
of subtle air.

DORIS LESSING

Her ears, lightly fringed with white that looked
silver, lifted and moved, back, forward, listening
and sensing. Her face turned, slightly, after
each new sensation, alert. Her tail moved, in
another dimension, as if its tip was catching
messages her other organs could not.
She sat poised, air-light, looking, hearing,
feeling, smelling, breathing, with all of
her, fur, whiskers, ears - everything, in
delicate vibration.

DORIS LESSING, b.1919

✧

Cats, no less liquid than their shadows,
Offer no angles to the wind.
They slip, diminished, neat, through loopholes
Less than themselves.

A.S.J. TESSIMOND (1902-1962)

✧

Chinese parents used to embroider a cat's head
on the shoes of a baby learning to walk, to make
it surefooted.

ISHA MELLOR

✧

DREAMING

The greater cats with golden eyes
Stare out between the bars.
Deserts are there, and different skies,
And night with different stars.

VITA SACKVILLE-WEST (1892-1962)

When Tabby crouches by the fire,
Primly agaze, her eyes are rings
Of agate flame: and strange desire
Burns there, and old unholy things.

When Tabby crouches by the fire,
Primly agaze, her eyes are rings
Of agate flame: and strange desire
Burns there, and old unholy things.

Surges on dream the lost Delight:
And off she goes, careering down
the windy archways of the night,
Afar on flying broomsticks blown.

R.W.D. FULLER

THE CAT WHO WALKS BY HIMSELF

Cat: a pygmy lion who
loves mice, hates dogs, and
patronizes human beings.

OLIVER HERFORD

It is a difficult matter to gain the affection of a
cat. He is a philosophical, methodical animal,
tenacious of his own habits, fond of order and
neatness, and disinclined to extravagant
sentiment. He will be your friend, if he finds
you worthy of friendship, but not your slave.

THEOPHILE GAUTIER (1811-1872)

Cat said, "I am not a friend, and I am not a
servant. I am the Cat who walks by himself, and
I wish to come into your Cave."

RUDYARD KIPLING (1865-1936)

A COMFORT TO US

Hear our prayer, Lord, for all animals,
May they be well-fed and well-treated
and happy:
Protect them from hunger and fear and
suffering:
And, we pray, protect specially, dear Lord,
The little Cat who is the companion of our home,
Keep her safe as she goes abroad,
And bring her back to comfort us.

AN OLD RUSSIAN PRAYER

Demanding - true; but also he
Deliberately sets out to be
A comfort in adversity.

GEORGE PARKER

One small cat changes coming home to an
empty house to coming home.

PAM BROWN

Once it has given its love, what absolute confidence, what fidelity of affection! It will make itself the companion of your hours of work, of loneliness, or of sadness. It will lie the whole evening on your knee, purring and happy in your society, and leaving the company of creatures of its own society to be with you.

THEOPHILE GAUTIER

ME AND THE CAT

We've seen so many winters come
and watched so many old years go
and held so many hands at dawn
we never really got to know.
Lying down someplace shady and flat,
me in my shirttails, him with his
whiskers
me and the cat.

·····• •·····

We've done so many foolish things
and yet the days have served us well.
We've given all our smiles away
when there were some we cared to sell.
Livin' the good life without gettin' fat,
me in my shirttails, him with his
whiskers
me and the cat.

·····• •·····

Looking back few friends had we
but I've got him and he's got me.

·····• •·····

And when the golden minute comes
when we no longer wake to smell
the river where the wild swans sailed
the orchard where the blossoms fell,
we'll smile a little thinkin' of that.
Me in my shirt-tails, him with his
whiskers
me and the cat.

ROD McKUEN

→←